A REFUGEE FOR LIFE

MEMOIRS OF RWANDA GENOCIDE SURVIVOR

ABAHO GIFT CONRAD

Memoirs of Rwanda Genocide Survivor
A Refugee For Life
by Abaho Gift Conrad
Frist Edition

Published by GL Design
3345 Chisholm Trail #206
Boulder, CO 80301

Copyright © 2021 by Abaho Gift Conrad

ISBN # 978-1-933983-28-8

Graphic Design and Layout:
Abaho Gift Conrad and Cameron Powers

Acknowledgements

My sincere appreciation goes to Musical Ambassadors of Peace, Ms. Jane Teresa Wouters, Ms. Charlotte Fuller and Ms. Jeanie Cotton for their encouragement.

4

Table of Contents

6

List of Acronyms

HHC..........Humanity Heart Charity

AIDS.........Acquired Immune Deficiency Syndrome

UNHCR......United Nations High Commission for Refugees

WFP.......... World Food Program

RTLM........Radio Televisión Libre de Mille Collines

STDS..........Sexually Transmitted Diseases

NGOs..........Non-government Organizations

Dedication

I dedicate this book to my Brother Edmund Ndemezo and my Son Kyan Abaho Gisa.

8

Life at Birth

I was born on December 25, 1992 in Gasabo, Rwanda where the 1994 Rwandan genocide elapsed from.

Mrs. Kaberuka, whom I had taken to be my mother, narrates: "On that fateful day of April 8, 1994, hateful news of killing Tutsi tribe members was spreading on the RTLM radio. It took less than 2 hours to see the killers come to our compound as if they had organized themselves earlier. They killed my husband and 5 other neighbors by cutting with a panga (machete) on the head and others on the neck. They all breathed their last quickly. I was hiding in the old latrine where I spent almost 5 hours. As I was watching, another group brought 3 kids and used the hoes to scatter their brains. After they left our house to go to the next neighbors, I decided to run to your father's house. Since he was a soldier and a cousin, I knew he would save us. But as I almost approached your house, I heard the screaming from inside. Then I ended up in the sorghum garden where I saw a little you sleeping. Both your dad and mum were butchered. I think your mother, after realizing that was her last day, feared that you would die with her. So she decided to hide the toddler you in the nearby sorghum garden. My son I am your aunt; not your biological mother as you think. Your mother and father must have died a very painful death. I looked at you as another burden at first. I thought if I hid with you, you would innocently scream and they would kill us. But then I remembered how your family had cared for us so I picked you up. To my surprise you never cried. This encouraged me to carry you on my back. We spent 6 days in that garden with a lot of stink from the corpses which could have been only 20 meters away from us."

Narrow Escape to Uganda

Mrs. Kaberuka continues: "From there we moved through the shrubs to the deepest jungles of Rulindo to Gicumbi where we found 8 more genocide survivors. Along Kageyo we heard continuous gunfire for almost 6 hours. We almost fell into an ambush but we kept in hiding for other 2 days until we finally heard no more gun shots. We followed River Mulindi where we saw many headless bodies. Water had turned into red because of human bodies and blood and it was full of stinking. We finally made it to Nyagatare where we joined a very big group of refugees and UNCHR trucks. We boarded with very many wounded people to Nakivale, Uganda."

Abaho Escape Route

Growing up in Nakivale Resettlement Camp

On reaching Nakivale, we were allocated a small unit of land. We had to construct our small wattle-made house first. My guardian started growing pumpkins, casava, beans and Irish potatoes. It was very hard for her to learn how to dig since she was from a cattle-keeping background but she had to endure and learn. I remember digging with her some days and sometimes I staying home. The camp was very over-populated so stealing our food from the garden was always a common incident. My guardian could also go to work in the gardens of the neighboring host community. She would do this often to bring food on the table. At the age of six I could also work as pancake vendor to support her and to buy some few scholastic materials.

My best Childhood Memories

Guhingira & Gushingira Give-away Ceremonies

This a day when the family would be giving away the food.

These were common in our village. Very many people would gather mostly on Saturdays and traditional dancers would be brought to entertain us.

A lot of food would be served and we could eat like there was no tomorrow. I would always regard Saturday as my best day.

Meeting at Fire Place: Gutarama

These were late evening small gatherings where the old people could tell us a lot of stories about who we are, where we came from, our culture traditions, and many other useful topics.

This where I met different childhood friends like Gahungu Fred, Emmanuel Gatete and Frank Mucyo.

Poetry: Kwivuga & Ukwivuga

These were poetic rapping competitions held every end of July.

They would be very interesting for us. We could learn more about our language in depth and how to compose songs in traditional natural tone. This could bring us together and could also bring a sense of belongingness among all the attendees. This helped us feel that we are one regardless of the conditions we are in.

General Community Cleaning Day: Serving Ubushera

The community leader would organize and make somedays, mostly every Thursday at the end of the month, to help in restoring sanitation in the camp. The water sources, roads and markets would be cleaned and rehabilitated.

Ubushera was a very common drink made from sorghum and millet. These two could be mixed to come up with a very tasty soft drink which would be given out for free to all people who got involved in general community cleanliness.

Hunting and Wild Fruit Gathering

We could form groups of 5 to go to the nearby bushes to pick wild fruits like berries and also we could go hunting small wild animals. We could come back home with some food which would be shared among different households.

Playing Football and Swimming

We could make our locally kavera or banana fiber-made balls. We could organize teams and we used to organize inter-village tournaments. I used to like striker position in most matches. As we grew up, I realized that swimming was my best sport, hence I began concentrating on swimming only.

School Times

I joined Nyarugugu primary school and studied there from primary one up to primary six, then shifted to Itegyero primary school. This was a better but far-away primary school and the main reason was to enable me get better grades. This improved my performance at school

Camp Hardships: Traumatized Community

In most Refugee Camps all over the world the refugees face similar challenges. Refugees displaced by war and genocide are the most traumatized ones. My experience was about genocide and ethnic cleansing. These make an individual always feel insecure especially the moment he or she meets someone from the enemy tribe. This can be confirmed by interviewing either Tutsi or Hutu from Rwanda or Burundi or Palestinians in West Bank or West Papuan in Indonesia etc.

Misuse of Drugs

Most youth in resettlement camps are jobless. This makes them lose hope and focus, hence we see them resorting to drugs as a way to forget about their challenges. This is worse in urban resettlement camps like in the Somali community in Kisenyi, Kampala.

Nakivale Refugee Camp

Hostile Governments

Some governments are very hostile to refugees. For example, during Obote's regime in Uganda, Rwandan refugees were seen as supporters of notorious NRA rebels. This created more hostility of tribes towards Rwandan Refugees. And the Tanzanian government under Kikwete in 1997 chased all the Rwandans back to Uganda or Rwanda.

High Level of Disease Outbreak

Due to poor health conditions, and high population density in most resettlement camps, diseases like Cholera, HIV/Aids, STDs, Dysentery, Flu, Common Cough and Malaria are common diseases affecting the refugee communities.

Bidi Bidi in northern Uganda is the World's Largest Camp

Hunger

Food is always the scarcest resource to most refugees in the world. For example the amount of food that the World food program/UNHCR gives to the registered refugees is only a quarter of the daily food needs of the host community. Some unregistered refugees go completely without food some days and living on an empty stomach is the order of the day.

Unhealthy Water Sources

During my stay in the camp, we would use stagnant water for drinking and cooking. Animals and humans used to share water sources and there was only one bore hole serving the entire community. Thanks to NGOs this has improved. However, this situation still exists in a few refugee resettlement camps like Nakivale and Bidi Bidi.

Water Sources in Bidi Bidi

High Crime Rates: Gender-Based Violence

The populations of most refugee resettlement camps are majorly composed of women and children. The major factors such as poverty, lack of education and livelihood opportunities, and impunity for crime and abuse, also tend to contribute to and reinforce a culture of violence and discrimination based on gender. In settlements such as Rhino Camp, Imvepi and Kyangwali, physical assault is the most reported incident. Among males, denial of resources and emotional abuse at the household level are the key incidents reported.

This is also due to over-population and inadequate jobs for refugee youth in these camps

Physical Safety and Security

UNHCR 2019 Legal and Protection Report

In Arua, there were 177 (107 refugee, 70 nationals) crimes reported during the month. Rhino camp with 122 cases (72 refugees, 50 nationals) recorded the highest number while Imvepi had 51 cases (34 refugees, 17 nationals) and Lobule had 4 (1 refugees and 3 nationals) cases.

In the three settlements of Arua, physical assault remained the highest reported crime case followed by theft, threatening of violence and domestic violence. Multi-sectoral protection interventions need to be strengthened to further reduce the rates of crime. The Arua operation has 89 (08 Lobule, 39 Imvepi and 42 Rhino) Community Watch Groups comprised of 343 members. The community watch members work in close collaboration with security secretaries in the Refugee Welfare Committee (RWC) structures of the respective villages. As a measure to register their effectiveness, the operation has embarked on plans to continue to support the structures through capacity building to ensure respect and dignity of the refugees and provide them with necessary facilities to serve in a timely manner.

In Rwamwanja, 16 (6Females/10Males) Persons of Concern (PoCs) are hosted in a protection house. They include 9 children (3Females/6Males) who are under a female care giver.

Sixty-six cases involving refugees were recorded at Kyangwali police station. Investigations were completed in 10 cases and the files were forwarded to the resident state attorney for perusal and advice. Thirteen were handled jointly with child and family protection unit and the SGBV (Sexual and Gender Based Violence) sector, as investigations are still ongoing in 43 cases. The nature of cases reported include disappearance, failure to provide, domestic violence, theft, assault, arson, loss of attestation cards, defilement, malicious damage of property, obtaining money by false pretence and other offences.

In Yumbe, the police were supported with stationary such as reams of paper, Police Forms and logistics for investigation, transportation of survivors/victims for medical examination and visiting scenes of crimes.

Additionally, 48 (25F/23M) cases were registered by the legal team in Yumbe. Thirty cases were successfully resolved and 18 were referred to police for further investigations and prosecution. The highest reported cases were assault (11), domestic violence (7), trespassing (7), theft (7), arson (5), child neglect (5), defilement (2), attempted suicide (2), and indecent assault (2). Four cases of combatants (males) in Zone 1 followed up their cases and were provided legal counseling and coordination with police.

Limited and Substandard Medical Facilities

The medical facilities are very few and also the high populations in the major resettlement camps overpowers the number of medical personnel at the available clinics. That is why during my childhood I grew up on herbs only. We couldn't get medicines easily and the only option was always to go the African way of use of herbs. There was only Rwamwanja Health Centre which has now been improved to Grade 3. In comparison to the 90s, it can now accommodate 70,000 refugees and 40,000 nationals.

Inadequate Schools

During my days there were only one substandard and very distant primary and secondary school. We could walk miles and miles to reach Nyarugugu and Nakivale primary schools which were also over-populated.

The host community had to share these facilities with the refugee community too.

Lack of Scholastic Materials

I remember one day I could not go to school because I had no books. Thank God one Reverend Rudahigwa gave me 2 of his short hand-books. The next day I reported to school. Books, pens, pencils, papers, school bags, uniforms are always a challenge to refugee school children.

Lack of School Fees

I was a very excellent student in class but always had worries of being blocked from class because of school fees. Not only was our school substandard but, worst still, we could not even afford the school fees and other scholastic materials. Definitely I am among the few 5 per cent of my lucky age-mates who managed to go to school.

Low Self-Esteem and Despair

When life puts you down you always feel inhuman and always you look at yourself unworthy of living. I experienced this since childhood up to the university level. Our general well-being could make us feel we are not human and we could feel despair most of the time. Most of the 1994 refugees joined government military forces not because of choice but due to despair. These were the Rwanda Patriotic Front (RPF or Front Patriotique Rwandais) which is now the ruling party of Rwanda and the National Resistance Army (NRA now named National Resistance Movement) which is now a ruling party in Uganda.

Giant Bidi Bidi Camp

Bullies at School

I studied during the time when the host community students would bully us and make us hate ourselves. We had to unite and form a group which could empower our fellow refugees to fight this stigma.

Joining Secondary School: My Godfather

My good grades attracted the chairperson on the board of school management. He started paying for me straight away from grade senior one. This changed my life completely. I had no more worries about being chased out because of failure to pay school fees on time. This also gave me the courage and determination to achieve my childhood dream. My performance changed because of this; I remember scoring 95 in almost all the fourteen subjects I had in grade senior one. This motivated me more and it was as if I had achieved my dream. I maintained this throughout ordinary level and also in advanced level where I took Math, Economics, Geography and Entrepreneurship. I chose this combination because it was aligned with my dream career of being a professional Accountant.

Tragic Moment: Sickness and Death of my Guardian

As soon as I stepped in senior five, my beloved guardias health started deteriorating. At first, we took her to hospital and she tested HIV positive, I felt completely heartbroken once again.

Before the year 2010 ended, she was again tested and to my surprise cancer had started eating her up. I could sit in class and imagine how she risked herself to rescue me. My six year in secondary was full of sorrows and heart breaks but I didn't give up on my dream. She finally passed away when I had just finished my Advanced level exams and was laid to rest on 15 February 2011.

Joining College in 2011 and Work Rejection

It was on 4th June when I got a call that I had been selected to do a diploma in business studies on full government sponsorship. This made me very happy and closer to my accounting dream. I had to report to Uganda college of commerce on 10th of July 2011 and my accounting journey started.

I had to spend sleepless nights reading and doing research to ensure that I came out with the best grades. Since my guardian was no more, I was somehow challenged with obtaining scholastic materials. I had to start looking for part-time teaching jobs. However whenever I went people would call me names: "Foreigner, foreigner, foreigner." This irritated me and made me lose hope for getting any teaching jobs in the country. However, I decided to keep focusing on the main dream which was accounting until I graduated in march 2013 with a second-class upper Diploma.

Reunion with my Relatives in Kigali

Immediately after graduating with a second class upper diploma from Uganda college of commerce, my mind had been yearning to go back to my motherland in Rwanda. My only remaining relatives in Kigali organized the bus fare for me to travel and meet them. On reaching there I reunited with some few remnant relatives. I moved around the whole country and my most interesting journey was going to Rwamagana, east of Kigali, to visit my ancestral place. It was fun and I felt at home but I didn't like how people there sarcastically called me a foreigner in my ancestral land.

I was called off shortly for a Data Assistant post at UNHCR Uganda, so I came back to Uganda and started working in data capturing. While working for UNHCR, I felt that there was a need to change lives of all the under-privileged. I organized a team of three like-minded friends who helped in the formation of HHC (Humanity Heart Charity) as Indatwa Association. We wanted to register as a non-profit but it was rejected without any clear reason. This shattered my dream of serving my fellow underprivileged.

With my Relatives in Kigali, Rwanda

New Job and Joining Makerere University

After working with UNHCR for a one-year contract, I landed an accounting job with Bol & company, a practicing Audit firm in Ntinda, Kampala, where I started as an Audit Assistant. The pay was very small but I had to keep pushing. After one year I enrolled for an evening program at Makerere University to pursue Bachelor of Commerce and I later certified as Forensic Auditor and Investigator. I could do these with around 4 extra part time jobs at Bravo Shoes Limited, Kabu Auctioneers, Star Limited and also Motase. That meant that I could sometimes do 3- 4 jobs a day and also attend evening lectures. All this could supplement my small income.

HHC Reformation and Registration

HHC (Humanity Heart Charity) is a social enterprise registered No. 80020002563503 in Uganda with the main purpose of improving lives of all the underprivileged people like refugees, blind, deaf, albinos, disabled, and orphans. It was founded in 2015 but became fully operational in 2019 for fellow underprivileged who went through the same hard life in resettlement camps.

HHC Field Team

What HHC (Humanity Heart Charity) Does

•   To provide sanitary items and basic utility items for all the underprivileged people.

•   To help in reducing trauma and provide free counseling services to all the refugees & underprivileged people.

•   To equip all the underprivileged people with vocational technical skills and language trainings.

•   To promote peace and reconciliation, restore hope, resolve inter-tribal and racial conflicts and unite all the people to ensure that they live in harmony.

•   To start up self-help projects for refugees and all underprivileged people to ensure that they can earn a living.

Why HHC?

We are focusing on sanitation which puts refugee lives at risk in all the over-populated camps. Health must be a right to every person.

We value mental healthcare, thus focusing on trauma which is the biggest threat to human lives, most especially those who have been in war.

We are giving these refugees skills to ensure that they can earn a living without entirely depending on the handouts.

We train in languages, social norms and customs so that refugees can live in harmony with other host communities.

Humanity Heart Charity recognizes that the handicapped are part of humanity.

Humanity Heart Charity bridges all these gaps to ensure that underprivileged have hope and can be proud that they are also part of the human race.

HHC Social Proof

• During the Covid outbreak, we realized that the refugee resettlement camps are very vulnerable to this so we had to create awareness and sensitization about the spread of corona virus. We supplied sanitary items which have curbed the spread. This reduced the risk of covid19 in camps. I can proudly say that there is no single case reported in refugee camps in Uganda as of December, 2021. Katusiime Allen is our HHC Field Coordinator.

• Our counseling team has helped to setup programs to encourage refugees to avoid drug abuse and instill hope. We are very proud of HHC Team. Ngabo Nicholas is our Youth Coordinator in Rwamwanja

• HHC helped in trauma reduction through music healing, counseling and reconciliation in Rwamwanja Camp. Christopher Rwahe is the Group leader of Mending the Broken Heart Group.

HHC Trauma Healing Session

HHCs Achievements 2019-2021

1.   We have managed to improve the health of the refugees in camps mostly Rwamwanja Camp by supplying free soap.

2.   We have ensured that refugees are aware of Covid and the way it spreads this has reduced the risks by 90% in refugee resettlement camp.

3.   We have organized a trauma healing and counseling team who call refugees and handle counseling sessions.

4.   We have so far organized 4 peace and reconciliation meetings between 3 different refugees' communities and the host community. This has ensured unity and harmony within the camp.

5.   We have so far covered 3 refugee resettlement camps in one year of operation. Those are Rwamwanja, Kyaka and Nakivale.

6.   Humanity Heart Ambassadors, we formed this arm of the charity which is doing tremendous field work through music healing and distribution of sanitary items.

7.   Motor vehicle mechanical workshop. We partnered with Aba Auto Centre and 3 underprivileged students are being trained on motor bike repairs. We are looking at increasing the number to 30 per shift.

Humanity Heart Charity Family

Why I Chose to Settle in Uganda

My Refugee Community

Uganda is one of the largest refugee host countries in the world with 1,400,000 refugees as per UNHCR Situational Report April 2020 and Wikipedia. There are over 11 camps in Uganda which include, Rwamwanja, Rhino Camp, Nakivale, Oruchinga, Bidibidi, Kyangwali, Acholi Pii, Impevi, Kyaka 1 and kyaka 2.

The refugees in these camps include Congolese, Sudanese, Somali, Eritreans, Ethiopians, Burundian and Rwandans. Uganda is a home to many refugees from different countries in Africa. There is a high refugee influx in Uganda and the number is increasing because of wars and other natural calamities. Therefore, every refugee would wish to stay in Uganda with fellow refugees.

My Refugee Family in Rwamwanja

My Culture:

Preference of Preserving Inyambo Cows

The love for my culture made me stay in Uganda. I like dressing traditionally and keeping local breeds of cows.

Uganda gave me an opportunity to do all these without any restriction.

Here we can preserve our Inyambarire (traditional dressing costume), Urugo Rwinka (cattle kraals) and Ukwivuga (poetry singing.)

Inyambo/Ankole Cows

Hospitality of the People

The majority of Ugandans are very hospitable in comparison with other African countries. Personally I experienced this on a daily basis therefore I had no reason to go to any other country.

The natural resources here include lakes, rivers, mountains, the equator, water falls, and hot springs. These factors make Uganda among the best destinations for any tourist to travel to.

I decided to stay here and enjoy these things too. You will find more about these in my book titled A Place to Travel to Before You Die. This gives a clear overview of why Uganda is among the best countries to travel to.

Source of the River Nile

Opportunities in Business, Farming

Small Cottage Industries

Uganda gave me an opportunity to carry out business and agriculture freely regardless of my original nationality. It gave me an opportunity for education too. It's easier for any foreigner to establish herself or himself in Uganda than in any other African country.

Various Tribes

Uganda has 56 tribes and about nine indigenous communities that formally came to be recognized in the 1995 constitutional amendment of 2005. English is the official language of Uganda. Luganda and Swahili are also widely spoken in most parts of the country. This makes it a diverse country for any foreigner to settle and mingle with the rest of the population. This also brings in cultural diversity among its citizens.

Former Indatwa

Conclusion

I wish to show the human race that hatred, despair, guns, bullets, diseases, hunger, and deprivation do not define us as human beings. Let us unite and make this planet a beautiful home for us all regardless of our tribe, race, religion, sex, etc

Hope, determination, courage, hard work, focus, enthusiasm, and faith have kept me moving and made me achieve my childhood dreams. Now my life goal is to empower fellow underprivileged people.

Nowadays my dream is to share love and that's why currently I am preaching and practicing about use of love as medicine.

If God blesses me enough to impact life of another person, then I would have truly lived. Be blessed!!!!!!

Appendices

Useful links. https://musicalambassadorsofpeace.org/abaho/

https://musicalambassadorsofpeace.org/uganda/

https://mail.google.com/mail/u/1?ui=2&ik=9316aa6cb7&attid=0.3&permmsgid=msg-a:r-8382937137985836277&th=1 7729039295d4454&view=att&disp=safe&realattid=17728fd 5572f0d5b285

https://youtu.be/CrXn5bxDZDE

https://youtu.be/A8IUo-QK8cc

https://drive.google.com/drive/folders/1nlLU5PLSsGInSfr-MAOacfL-rGtR4e1gT?usp=sharing.

https://www.facebook.com/Humanity-Heart-Charity-580120662680055

https://thisismy.ngo/humanityheartcharity

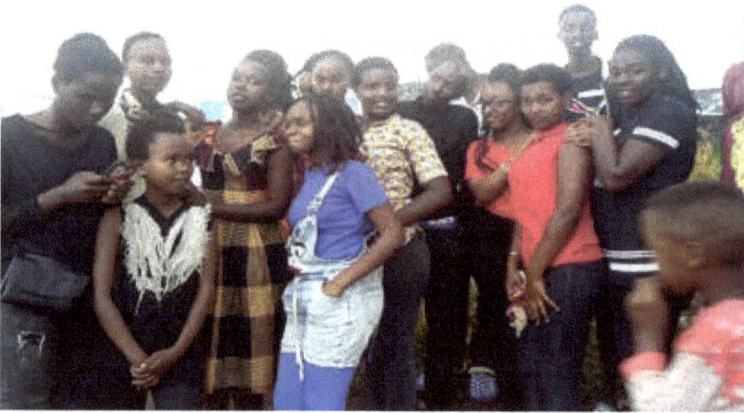

World Youth Day in Rwamwanja Camp

Author: Abaho Gift Conrad

Reference Books

1. A Place to Travel to Before You Die

2. Healing the Wounded World

3. Being a Man

4. UNHCR Situational Report April 2020

www.ingramcontent.com/pod-product-compliance
Lightning Source LLC
Chambersburg PA
CBHW071449040426
42445CB00012BA/1489